A MUSICAL APPLICATION OF
RUDIMENTS TO THE DRUMSET

BY JOE MORELLO

Original text edited by Marvin Dahlgren
Original examples transcribed by Armand Santarelli
Reissue layout by Gerald Vitale
Music engraving by Willie Rose

International Copyright Secured
Published by: Modern Drummer Publications, Inc.
271 Route 46 West Suite H-214
Fairfield, New Jersey 07004

www.moderndrummer.com

This book is a reissue of Joe Morello's previously out-of-print
classic *Rudimental Jazz: A Modern Application Of The Rudiments
To The Drum Outfit*, originally released in 1967.

CONTENTS

FOREWORD

We drummers are a resourceful lot. With the invention of the contraption we've come to call the drumset, we see an early version of "corporate downsizing." The drumset allowed one man to do a "job," in this case to play a march, which previously took three men—a snare drummer, a bass drummer, and a cymbal player. From the very beginning, the military roots of the drumset were obvious.

But "rudimental jazz"? Really? Sounds like an oxymoron—*rudimental* suggests something prescribed and rigid, while *jazz* suggests something free and flowing. How can they go together?

When Joe Morello released his third book, *Rudimental Jazz*, back in 1967, the previous offerings being *New Directions In Rhythm* and *Off The Record*, all questions about how the rudiments could be applied in a non-military setting were answered.

Why do we still play paradiddles, and continue to find new ways to express our musical ideas through paradiddles, today? We are still playing paradiddles because that particular sticking, like each of the rudiments, is not a "style" but an incredibly efficient *and* malleable drumming "scale."

In his introduction, Joe states, "My early training was based on a *rudimental* approach to my instrument." He says the rudiments are "the 'scales' of drumming," and that "this foundation has helped a great deal in later technical development." Of course! In the hands of a musically creative person, the rudiments are as valid and useful, and are as much a source for developing a personal voice on the instrument today, as they were a hundred years ago.

When I was a kid, I thought every drummer I heard was creating his own language on the drumset. One of my first idols was Carmine Appice. I especially liked his soloing on the tom-toms. A couple years later I discovered Gene Krupa and was initially struck by how much his solos reminded me of Carmine's; in fact, I thought Gene stole Carmine's licks! When I realized Gene was playing that way thirty years before Carmine and that the influence had been the other way around, I began to hear the common drum language between Gene, the jazz drummer, and Carmine, the rock drummer—the rudiments.

A few years later, in 1971, I had the good fortune to begin my studies with Joe Morello. We focused primarily on developing fluid hand technique, but Joe would also sprinkle in some coordination exercises using variations on *Stick Control* and *Syncopation*. After a few months he told me I was ready to get his book *Rudimental Jazz*. I still have my original copy of the

Paul La Raia

book with Joe's lesson notes in broad Sharpie on each page.

By working at that material I saw the obvious connection between the rudiments and flowing movements around the kit. I could hear phrases that reminded me not only of Gene Krupa and Buddy Rich but also of the "current" drummers I was checking out at that time: Max Roach, Philly Joe Jones, Billy Cobham, and David Garibaldi. In playing through *Rudimental Jazz* again now, I'm finding phrases that remind me of Bill Stewart, Eric Harland, Ari Hoenig, Vinnie Colaiuta, and Jeff Watts!

Yes, the rudiments work great in a military context; they are also applicable in an orchestral context. Joe Morello is a jazz drummer, so *Rudimental Jazz* explores the exact same rudiments in a jazz context. But the reality is that you can play Joe's orchestrations of the rudiments in any groove you want, so the book really could be titled *Rudimental Rock*, *Rudimental Funk*, *Rudimental Hip-Hop*, and so on. The rudiments are the scales, and in *Rudimental Jazz* Joe provides us with a great collection of fluid, melodic orchestrations of those scales. Check it out—I'm sure your playing, regardless of your choice of musical style, will benefit.

John Riley, January 2010

INTRODUCTION

There has been much discussion and argument—pro and con—among the drumming fraternity as to the real value of the drum rudiments. The main argument raised by those opposed to the rudiments is that they were intended for marching drummers and have no application in modern rock or jazz. I cannot go along with this argument at all, for my early training was based on a rudimental approach to my instrument, and I feel this foundation helped a great deal in my later technical development.

The rudiments are exercises for developing control and technique for the solo drummer. They should be a part of every drummer's early training. Their study is a foundation on which to build complete technical and musical command of the instrument. The basic rudiments were established by N.A.R.D. (the National Association For Rudimental Drummers) in 1933. Drummers shouldn't restrict their rudimental study to just the basic thirteen or twenty-six "standard American" rudiments. Drummers should explore the endless possible variations of each rudiment or create some new ones.

Drum rudiments are simply combinations of the three stick movements: the single stroke, the double stroke (stroke and rebound), and the flam. With these three basic movements, you can create thousands of interesting rhythmic patterns or exercises.

SINGLE STROKE

A single stroke is exactly what its name implies: one isolated note struck with a single stick. It will vary from a very soft grace note of approximately 2 inches to a 6-inch tap to a 12-inch half stroke, all the way up to a full stroke, which often involves producing an arch from the tip of the stick of over 24 inches.

DOUBLE STROKE

The double stroke is two notes struck with the same stick. It will vary from a pair of soft notes from a 2-inch height to a height that is limited only by your ability at the speed at which you're playing. As you increase the speed, you should control the initial stroke and allow the stick to rebound once.

FLAM

A flam is two notes played almost simultaneously with both sticks. The first note is a grace note. The second note is the principal stroke and is played a little louder. For proper production of the flam, think of both sticks starting for the drum at the same time, only the stick that plays the grace note starts from a position closer to the drumhead. The flam is used to reinforce or add body to the stroke and derives its name from the sound that it produces when executed. The grace note has no time value and is played within the rhythm of the primary note.

RUDIMENTS CAN SWING

It is true that the basic concept of drum rudiments was for military music. However, rudiments can be easily adapted to the drumset. The rudiments selected for this book include the thirteen essential rudiments, as well as several others that fit the jazz idiom. By using your imagination, any rudiment can be made to swing.

EXPLANATION OF NOTATION

All rudiments are referred to as right-hand or left-hand rudiments depending on which hand plays the first principal note. If a rudiment starts with grace notes, the grace notes are not considered when naming the rudiment. The primary stroke immediately after the grace note determines if it is a right- or left-hand rudiment.

Examples:
A right-hand paradiddle

A left-hand five-stroke roll

A right-hand flam

A left-hand drag

In jazz, the grace notes of ruffs, drags, and ratamacues are often played as taps or half strokes. Another liberty taken by modern drummers is to treat the grace notes as open and give them a time value equal to the other notes in the rudiment. Even though these distortions of the grace notes take place, they do not change the name of the sticking of the rudiment.

Here's a right-hand single ratamacue using a traditional interpretation.

Here's a variation used by many jazz drummers.

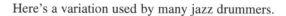

KEY

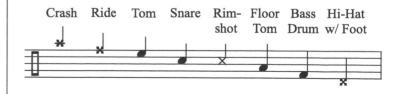

SINGLE-STROKE ROLL

A single-stroke roll is a simple alternation of sticks: RLRLRL. It should be practiced starting with either hand.

When played with accents, the single-stroke roll becomes a valuable tool for jazz drummers.

SINGLE-STROKE ROLL IN 8TH NOTES

SINGLE-STROKE ROLL IN 8TH-NOTE TRIPLETS

SINGLE-STROKE ROLL IN 16TH NOTES

SINGLE-STROKE ROLL AROUND THE DRUMSET

Play four measures of time before each exercise.

Notice that the bass drum is played on all four beats of the measure and the hi-hat is played on the second and fourth beats. Maintain those patterns in all exercises in 4/4, unless written otherwise.

1

R L R L R L R L   R L R L R   R L R L R L R L   R L R L R L R

8TH-NOTE TRIPLETS AROUND THE KIT

2

R L R L R L R L R L R L   R L R L R L R L R L   L R L R L R L R L R   R L R L R L R L R L R L

16TH NOTES AROUND THE KIT

3

R L R L R L R L R L R L R L R   R L R L R L R L R L R L R L R L R

R L R L R L R L R L R L R L R L R L   R L R L R L R L R L R L R L R L R

CROSS-STICKING

Cross-sticking is a technique for getting from one drum to another without breaking the flow of rhythm, where one stick passes over the other while proceeding to a different drum. For example, the left hand crosses over the right hand to go to a drum on the right side of the kit, and the right hand crosses over the left hand to go to a drum that's to the left. Cross-stickings are used throughout this book, and the hand that does the crossover is marked with an "x."

Cross left stick over right   Cross right stick over left

4

R L R L R L R L R L   L R L R L R L R L R   R L R L R L R L R L R L   R L R L R L R L R L R L

5

R L R L R L R L R L R L   R L R L R L R L R L R L   R L R L R L R L R L R L   R L R L R L R L R L R L

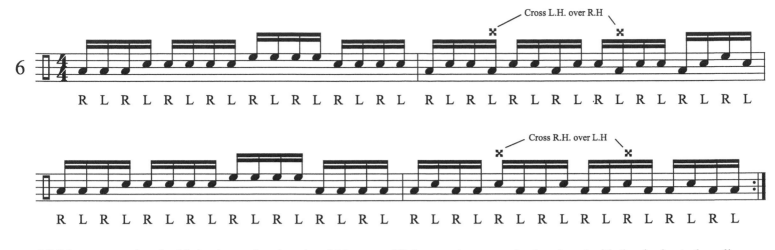

6

All 8th-note exercises in this book may be played as 16th notes. All the exercises may also be played with the single-stroke roll.

LONG ROLL

As often written:

A long roll consists of alternating double strokes. The second note is accented to build finger and wrist strength.

L   L   R   R   L   L   R   R   L L R R etc.

You should be adept at starting the long roll with either hand. The long-roll exercises in this book are planned to end with the right hand going to the cymbal. Each exercise is to be preceded by four measures of time.

LONG ROLL IN 8TH NOTES

Play the bass drum on all four beats and the hi-hat on beats 2 and 4.

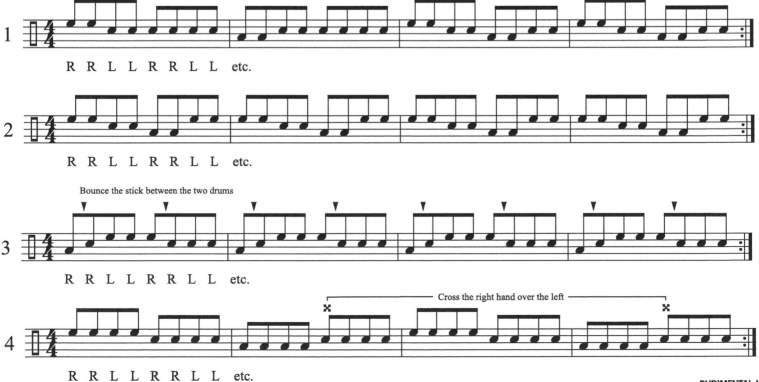

1

R   R   L   L   R   R   L   L   etc.

2

R   R   L   L   R   R   L   L   etc.

Bounce the stick between the two drums

3

R   R   L   L   R   R   L   L   etc.

Cross the right hand over the left

4

R   R   L   L   R   R   L   L   etc.

The following three exercises are based on an 8th-note long roll that has the first note of each double stroke on the offbeat.
Precede each exercise with four measures of time.

1

L R R L L R R L etc.

2

L R R L L R R L etc.

3

L R R L L R R L etc.

Keep a notebook handy. Write down ideas as they occur to you, using your imagination to develop your own bag of tricks.

LONG ROLL IN TRIPLET FORM (LONG-ROLL TRIPLET)

A long-roll triplet combines the rhythm of triplets with the sticking of a long roll. Each exercise is to be preceded by four measures of time.

1

R R L L R R L L R R L L etc.

2

R R L L R R L L R R L L etc.

3

R R L L R R L L R R L L etc.

4

R R L L R R L L R R L L etc.

5

R R L L R R L L R R L L etc.

6
R R L L R R L L R R L L etc.

7
R R L L R R L L R R L L etc.

8
R R L L R R L L R R L L etc.

9
R R L L R R L L R R L L etc.

10
R R L L R R L L R R L L etc.

11
R R L L R R L L R R L L

12
R R L L R R L L R R L L etc.

13
R R L L R R L L R R L L etc.

14
R R L L R R L L R R L L etc.

The rhythm of long-roll triplets may be written under two triplet signs per measure instead of four. Play the bass drum on all four beats and the hi-hat on beats 2 and 4.

1
R R L L R R L L R R L L etc.

The following three exercises are written to give you a chance to practice feeling six pulses in the hands against four beats in the bass drum.

2   R R L L R R L L R R L L etc.

3   R R L L R R L L R R L L etc.

4   R R L L R R L L R R L L etc.

Practicing the exercises in this book should inspire you to invent your own. Write them down! It's very important to develop a vocabulary of your own ideas.

LONG ROLL IN 16TH NOTES

Each exercise is to be preceded by four measures of time.

1   R R L L R R L L R R L L R R L L etc.

2   R R L L R R L L R R L L R R L L etc.

3   R R L L R R L L R R L L R R L L

etc.

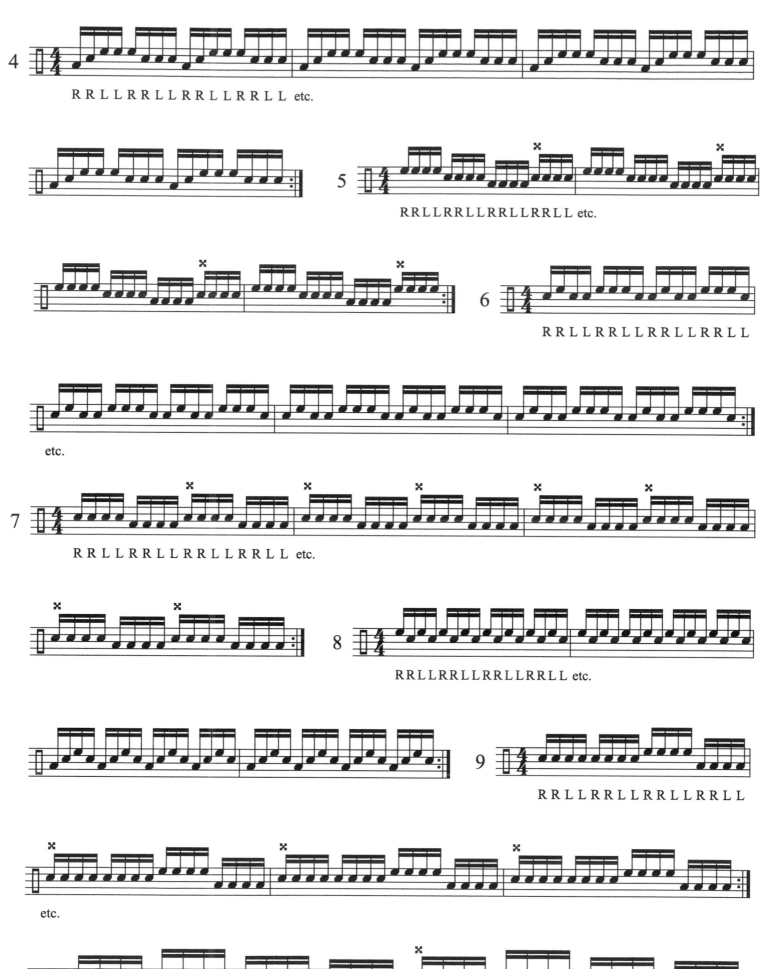

4 RRLLRRLLRRLLRRLL etc.

5 RRLLRRLLRRLLRRLL etc.

6 RRLLRRLLRRLLRRLL

etc.

7 RRLLRRLLRRLLRRLL etc.

8 RRLLRRLLRRLLRRLL etc.

9 RRLLRRLLRRLLRRLL

etc.

10 RRLLRRLLRRLLRRLL etc.

SINGLE PARADIDDLE

A single paradiddle is four notes sticked either RLRR or LRLL (two single strokes and a double). It is named *paradiddle* because that approximates its sound.

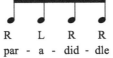

R   L   R   R
par - a - did - dle

RLRR is called a right-hand paradiddle. LRLL is called a left-hand paradiddle. When successive paradiddles are played, they alternate (a right-hand paradiddle followed by a left-hand paradiddle).

The traditional placement for an accent in the single paradiddle is on the first note.

Jazz drummers freely accent other notes, however, and are just as accomplished at playing the single paradiddle in the following manner:

Accent on the second note

Accent on both single strokes

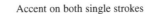

Accenting the first note of one paradiddle and the second note of the other

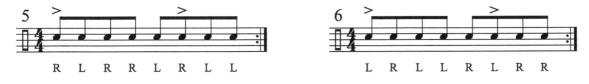

More difficult to master but equally effective when accomplished are paradiddles with accents on either one or both of the double strokes.

Another widely used device is the permutation of the single paradiddle. This means starting the paradiddle on a subdivision of the beat other than the downbeat.

Combining double accents with permutations gives you the following exercises:

Strive to be able to play 200 or more paradiddles (straight or permutated) in one minute.

When practicing the permutations at maximum speed, try to place the first note of the paradiddle on the proper part of the beat, and feel the rest of the paradiddle exactly as you do when it is started on the beat. The maximum speed that you can play the permutations of the paradiddle will be the rate at which your mind is capable of feeling the different parts of the beat. Therefore, train yourself to think quickly and divide time precisely.

COMBINING PARADIDDLES WITH TRIPLETS

8th-note triplets played with paradiddle stickings are called 8th-note paratriplets.

If the traditional accent of the first beat of the paradiddle is used, the accent will form the rhythm of a half-note triplet. This is important to know for speed of execution.

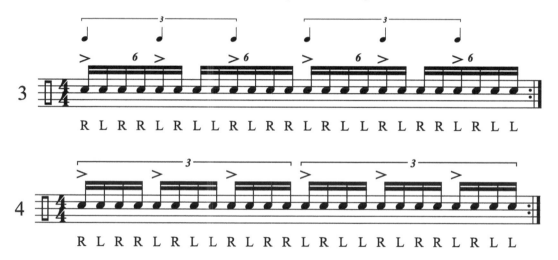

16th-note triplets with paradiddle stickings are called 16th-note paratriplets. When played with the accent on the first note of the paradiddles, the rhythm of the accents will be quarter-note triplets.

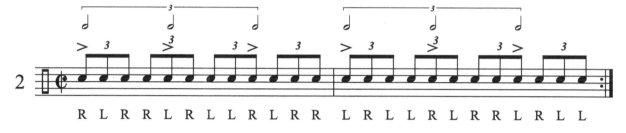

Your speed of execution will improve if you think of the rhythm of quarter-note triplets and play a paradiddle on each of the six pulses in one measure of 4/4. Combining different rhythms and accents on paradiddles makes it possible to invent countless interesting phrases.

PARADIDDLES AROUND THE DRUMSET

The following exercises will give you many ideas for spreading the paradiddle and paratriplet around the drumset.
Each exercise is to be preceded by four measures of time. The bass drum is played on all four beats and the hi-hat
is played on the second and fourth beat, unless written otherwise.

1 R L R R L R L L etc.

2 R R L R L L R L etc.

3 R L L R L R R L etc.

4 R L R R L   L R   L L R   R L R R   L   L R L L

5 R L R R L R L L etc.

6 R L R R L R L L etc.

7 R L R R L R L L etc.

8 R L   R   R   L R L L   R L   R   R   L R L L

9 L R   L   L   R L R R   L R   L   L   R L R R

18

R L R R L R   L L R L R R   L R L L R L   R R L R L L

19

R L R R L R   L L R L R R   L R L L R L   R R L R L L

Exercises 20, 21, and 22 are executed with the bass drum playing with the cymbal.

20

R L R R L R L L R L R R   L R L L R L R R L R L L   R L R R L R L L R L R R

L R L L R L R R L R L L

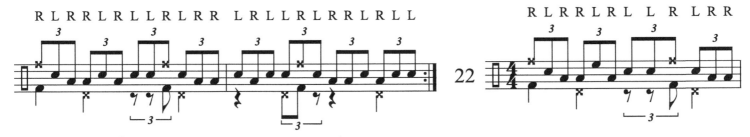

21

R L R R L R L   L R   L R R   L R L L R L R R L R L L

R L R R L R L L R L R R   L R L L R L R R L R L L

22

R L R R L R L L   L R   L R R

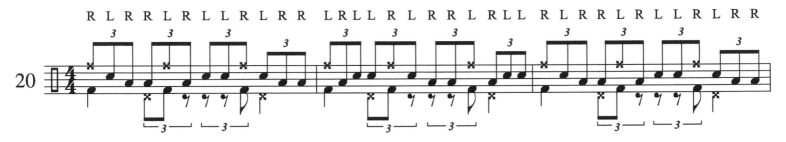

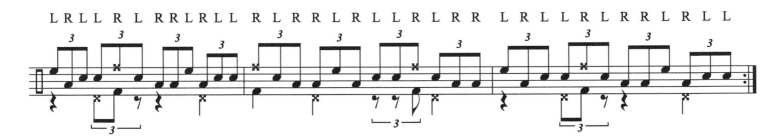

L R L L R L R R L R L L   R L R R L R L L R L R R   L R L L R L R R L R L L

Exercise 23 is an eight-measure solo.

23

R L R R   L R L L   R L R R   L R L L   R L R R L R L L R L R R   L R L L R L R R L R L L

R L R R   L R L L   R L R R   L R L L   R L R R L R L L R L R R   L R L L R L R R L R L L

FIVE-STROKE ROLL

The five-stroke roll consists of two double strokes followed by a single stroke.

L L R R L R R L L R L L R R L R R L L R etc.

Each exercise is to be preceded by four measures of time.

1 L L R R L R R L L R L L R R L R R L L R L L R R L R R L L R L L

L L R R L R R L L R L L R R L R R L L R L L R R L R R L L R L L R R L R R L L R L L R R L R R L L

3 L L R R L R R L L R L L R R L R R L L R L L R R L R R L L R L L

4 R R L L R L L R R L R R L L R R R L L R

5 R R L L R L L R R L R R L L R L L R R L

6 R R L L R L L R R L R R L L R L L R R L R R L L R L L R R L R R L L R

7 R R L L R L L R R L etc.

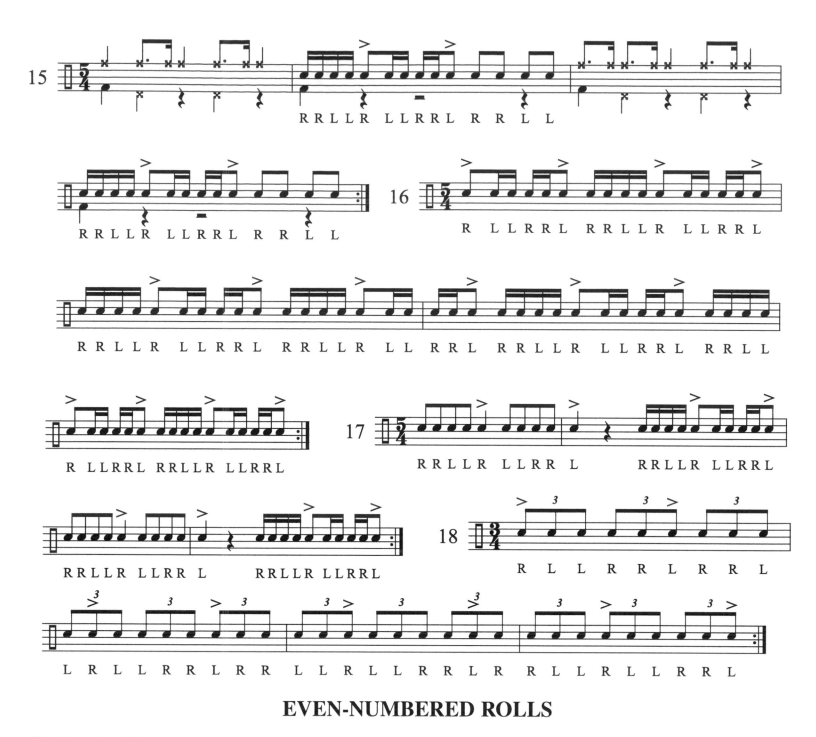

EVEN-NUMBERED ROLLS

The six-stroke roll is a combination of two double strokes and two single strokes. All even-numbered rolls (six-stroke, eight-stroke, ten-stroke, etc.) end with two single strokes (usually accented).

The Six-Stroke Roll

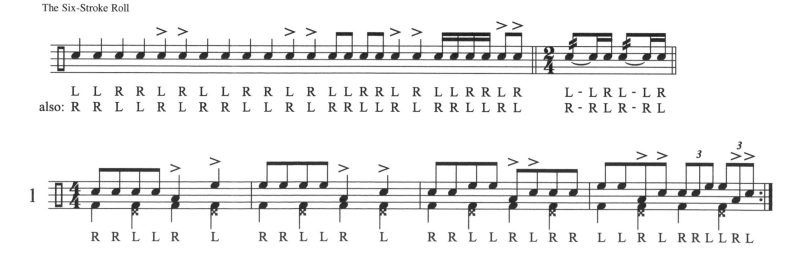

2

RLLRRLRLLRRL R   RRLLRL RLLRRLR RLL RRLR RRLLRL

3

RRLLR L RRLLRL L R LLRRL R LLRRL R   LLRRL R   RRLLRLRRLLR L

The syncopated bass drum in Exercise 4 is for advanced drummers.

R   R RL   LRL   L   L   R   RLR   RRLLRL R   RL   LRL   RRLLRL   RRL

4

5

R L L R R L etc.

Try similar phrases on your drumset using the eight- and ten-stroke roll.

Eight-Stroke Roll

L   L   R   R   L   L   R   L

Ten-Stroke Roll

L   L   R   R   L   L   R   R   L   R

SEVEN-STROKE ROLL

The seven-stroke roll consists of three double strokes and one single stroke. Like all short rolls, it's a derivative of the long roll.

etc.

L L R R L L R L L R R L L R L L R R L L R L L R R L L R etc.
also: R R L L R R L R R L L R R L R R L L R R L R R L L R R L etc.

Each exercise is to be preceded by four measures of time.

NINE-STROKE ROLL

The nine-stroke roll is composed of four double strokes and one single stroke. Alternate this rudiment.

RRLLRRLLR   LLRRLLRRL   R R L L R R L L R   L L R R L L R R L

Each example is to be preceded by four bars of time.

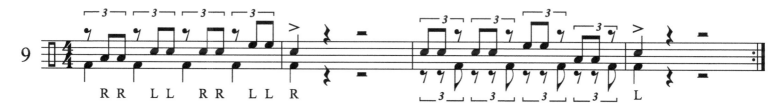

FLAM

The traditional flam is a principal note played from a high position preceded by a grace note played from a low position.
The sound of a flam is a thick one ranging from "fa-lam" at the slow beginning stage to the sound of the word *flam* at the fast advanced stage. Take care that the grace note always strikes first and that you get a full, thick sound, regardless of how fast you play flams or flam rudiments.

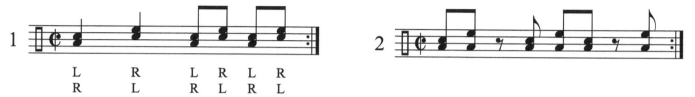

etc. closed and open

lR   rL   lR   rL   lR rL lR rL lR rL lR   rL lR rL lR rL

FLAT FLAM

The flat flam is not one of the twenty-six standard rudiments. It is played by having both sticks strike at the same time.
For drumset players, this rudiment is used when two different drums are being played simultaneously.
 In Exercise 1, the right hand travels between two toms. In Exercise 2, the left hand travels between the snare drum and the small tom.

1 L R L R L R
   R L R L R L

2

In jazz, we alternate the rudimental flam only if doing so makes it more convenient to move around the drumset.

3 lR lR rL lR   rL lR lR   lR   lR rL rL   lR rL   lR rL   rL

4

FLAM TAP

A flam tap is a flam followed by a single stroke. The single stroke is played from a low position, which is why it's referred to as a tap.

lR   R rL L lR RrL L   lR RrL LlR RrL L   lR RrL LlR RrL L

Each exercise is to be preceded by four measures of time.

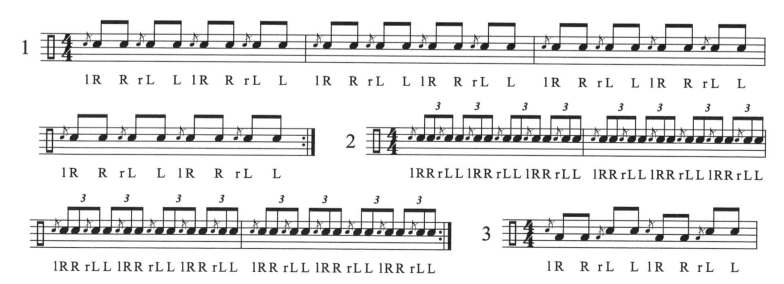

1 lR R rL L lR R rL L   lR R rL L lR R rL L   lR R rL L lR R rL L

lR R rL L lR R rL L

2 lRR rLL lRR rLL lRR rLL lRR rLL lRR rLL lRR rLL

lRR rLL lRR rLL lRR rLL lRR rLL lRR rLL lRR rLL

3 lR R rL L lR R rL L

FLAM ACCENT

A flam accent is a flam followed by two single strokes. The rudiment alternates.

1R   L   R   rL   R   L   1R   L   R   rL   R   L   1R   L   R   rL   R   L etc.

Precede each exercise with four measures of time. Flams on multiple surfaces can be played as flat flams.

FLAMACUE

The flamacue comprises a flam, an accented single stroke, two unaccented single strokes (called taps), and another flam. The flamacue is one of the most difficult rudiments to perform. The difficulty lies in the fact that the accented second note is played with the same hand that plays the grace note of the beginning flam.

Practice the following exercise to overcome this difficulty. Relax your wrist on the unaccented note, and allow your elbow to move away from your body. Quickly move your elbow in to help throw your wrist up, and immediately snap the wrist down for the accent. This action puts the weight of the upper arm behind the accented note.

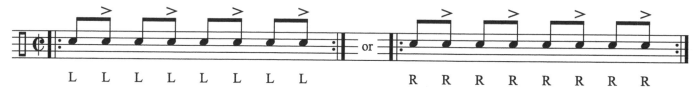

Adjacent flamacues will share the same flam.

1

   lR   L   R   L   lR   L   R   L   lR   L   R   L   lR

2

lR L R L lR L R L lR L R L   lR L R L lR L R L lR L R L

This exercise has a more complex bass drum pattern for advanced players.

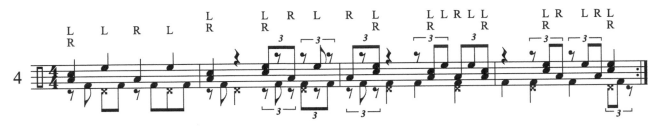

3

4

5

L L L R L L L R L R L L L R L L R L R L L L R L L R L R L L R L
R   R   R   R   R   R   R   R

SINGLE FLAM PARADIDDLE

lR   L   R   R rL R   L   L   lR L R R rL R L L lR L R R rL R L L

etc.

Each exercise is to be preceded by four measures of time.

1

lR L R R rL R L L   lR L R R rL R L L   lR L R R rL R L L

lR L R R rL R L L

2

lRLRRrLRLL lRLRR rLRLL lRLRRrLRLL

lRLRRrLRLLlRLRR rLRLLlRLRRrLRLL

3

lR L R R rL R L L

lR L R R rL R L L   lR L R R rL R L L   lR L R R rL R L L

The phrasing in Exercises 12–14 is a three-beat idea within a phrase of four measures of 4/4 time.

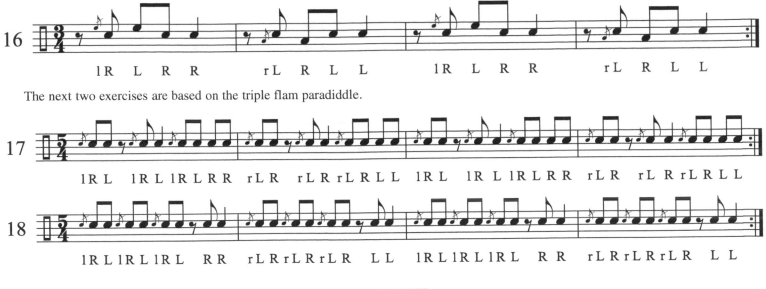

16 | 1R L R R | rL R L L | 1R L R R | rL R L L

The next two exercises are based on the triple flam paradiddle.

17 | 1R L 1R L 1R L R R rL R rL R rL R L L | 1R L 1R L 1R L R R rL R rL R rL R L L

18 | 1R L 1R L 1R L R R rL R rL R rL R L L | 1R L 1R L 1R L R R rL R rL R rL R L L

RUFF

The ruff consists of a double stroke and a single stroke. In traditional rudimental playing, the double stroke is played as two grace notes. This is followed immediately with a single stroke.

1lR   rrL   1lR   rrL

In jazz, the ruff is alternated for convenience when moving around the drumset.

1 | 1 1R   1 1R   r r L   1 1R | r r L   1 1R   1 1R   r r L   1 1

It is also played as a three-stroke ruff using three single strokes.

2 | 1 r L   1 r L   r 1 R   1 r L | r 1 R   1 r L   1 r L   r 1 R   r 1

The rudiment can be extended to a four-stroke ruff if you want an even fuller sound.

3 | 1r1R   1r1R   r1rL   1r1R | r1rL   1r1R   1r1R   r1rL

The grace notes of the ruff and ruff rudiments (single drag; double drag; single, double, and triple ratamacues) are sometimes played so open (slow) that they take on the value and volume of the other notes in the phrase.

Here are some examples.

4 | R R L   R R L   R R L   R R L | L L R   L L R   L L R   L L
       Ruff

5 | L R L L R L L R | L L R L L R L L | R R L R R L R R | L R R L R R L L
         Ruff

6 | RRLRRLRRLRRL | RRLRRLRRLRRL | RRLRRLRRLRRL | RLLRLLRRL

SINGLE DRAG

A single drag is a ruff and a single stroke. The right-hand ruff is followed by a left-hand single stroke. The left-hand ruff is followed by a right-hand single stroke. Alternate this rudiment.

Each exercise is to be preceded by four measures of time.

DOUBLE DRAG

Each exercise is to be preceded by four measures of time.

Note: Exercises 4–10 may be played in triplet and 16th-note form.

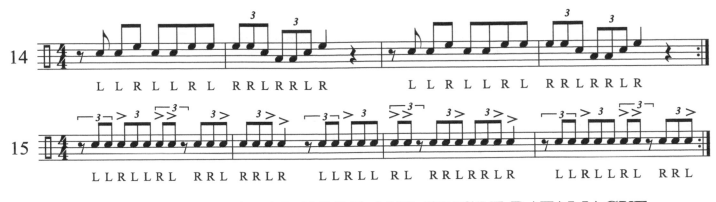

14

L L R L L R L   R R L R R L R   L L R L L R L   R R L R R L R

15

L L R L L R L   R R L   R R L R   L L R L L   R L   R R L R R L R   L L R L L R L   R R L

DOUBLE PARADIDDLE AND SINGLE RATAMACUE

The next two rudiments are the double paradiddle and the single ratamacue. Both comprise six notes.

Double Paradiddle

1

R L R L R R   L R L R L L

Single Ratamacue

2

l l R   L R L   r r L   R L R

If the grace notes of the single ratamacue are played open enough to have the same rhythm as the single notes, the rudiment becomes identical in sticking to the double paradiddle.

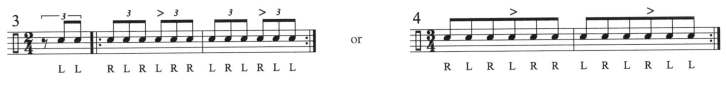

3

L L   R L R L R R   L R L R L L

or

4

R L R L R R   L R L R L L

An interesting phrase results when the accents of both rudiments are combined.

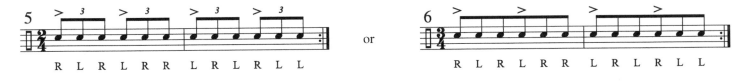

5

R L R L R R   L R L R L L

or

6

R L R L R R   L R L R L L

The next exercise combines the double paradiddle and the single ratamacue.

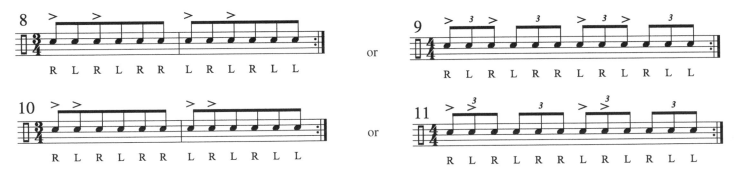

7

R L R L R R L R L R L L   R R L R L R L L R L R L

Other accents commonly employed with the double paradiddle are:

8

R L R L R R   L R L R L L

or

9

R L R L R R   L R L R L L

10

R L R L R R   L R L R L L

or

11

R L R L R R   L R L R L L

For additional practice, permutate all of the exercises in this section. The following are examples.

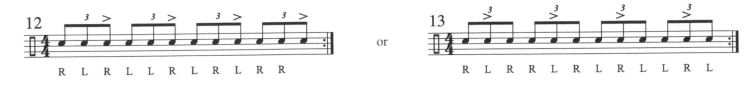

12

R L R L L R L R L R R

or

13

R L R R L R L R L L R L

DOUBLE PARADIDDLE

Each exercise is to be preceded by four measures of time.

SINGLE RATAMACUE

1lR L R L rrL R L R 1lRLRL rrLRLR 1lRLRL rrLRLR etc.

Each exercise is to be preceded by four measures of time.

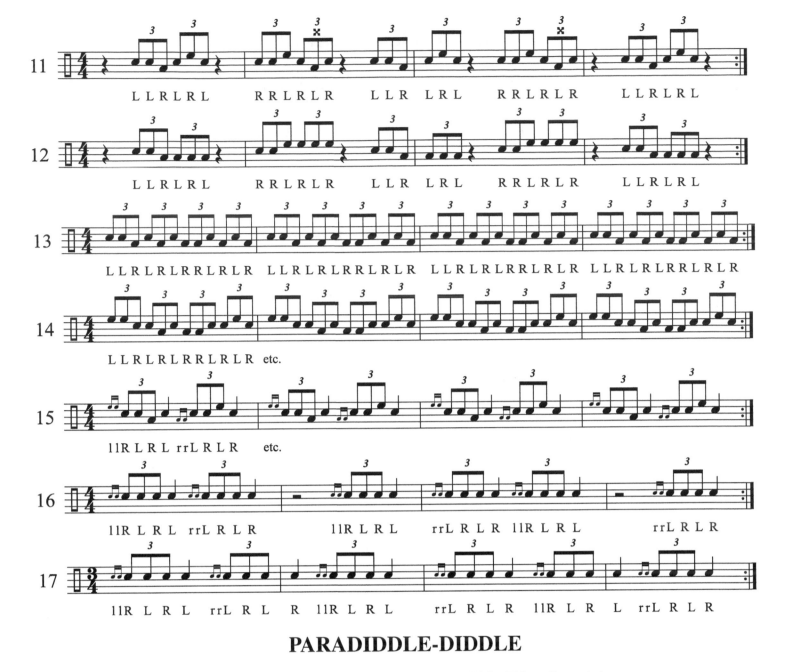

11

L L R L R L   R R L R L R   L L R   L R L   R R L R L R   L L R L R L

12

L L R L R L   R R L R L R   L L R   L R L   R R L R L R   L L R L R L

13

L L R L R L R R L R L R   L L R L R L R R L R L R   L L R L R L R R L R L R   L L R L R L R R L R L R

14

L L R L R L R R L R L R   etc.

15

1lR L R L   rrL R L R   etc.

16

1lR L R L   rrL R L R   1lR L R L   rrL R L R   1lR L R L   rrL R L R

17

1lR   L R L   rrL R L   R   1lR L R L   rrL R L R   1lR L R   L   rrL R L R

PARADIDDLE-DIDDLE

Another six-note sticking that's used a great deal in modern jazz is the paradiddle-diddle. This rudiment is important
because of its speed and ease of execution due to the two double strokes it contains. The paradiddle-diddle does not alternate.

1

R L R R L L   R L R R L L

Paradiddle-diddles starting with the left hand are great for developing the weaker hand.

2

L R L L R R   L R L L R R

Two 16th-note paradiddle-diddles fill up one measure of 3/4 time and can be permutated to create more difficult exercises.

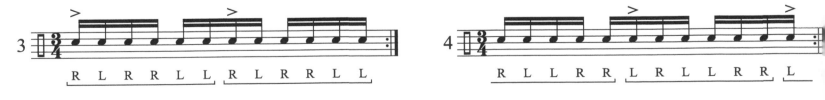

3

R L R R L L   R L R R L L

4

R L L R R   L R L L R R   L

Two paradiddle-diddles combined with two paradiddles will complete one measure of 5/4.

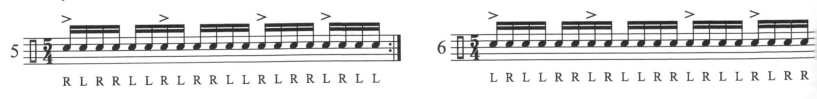

5

R L R R L L R L R R L L R L R R L R L L

6

L R L L R R L R L L R R L R L L R R L R R

Another interesting and useful sticking results if you change the last double stroke to an accented single stroke.

Try these exercises:

TRIPLE PARADIDDLE

Each exercise is to be preceded by four measures of time.

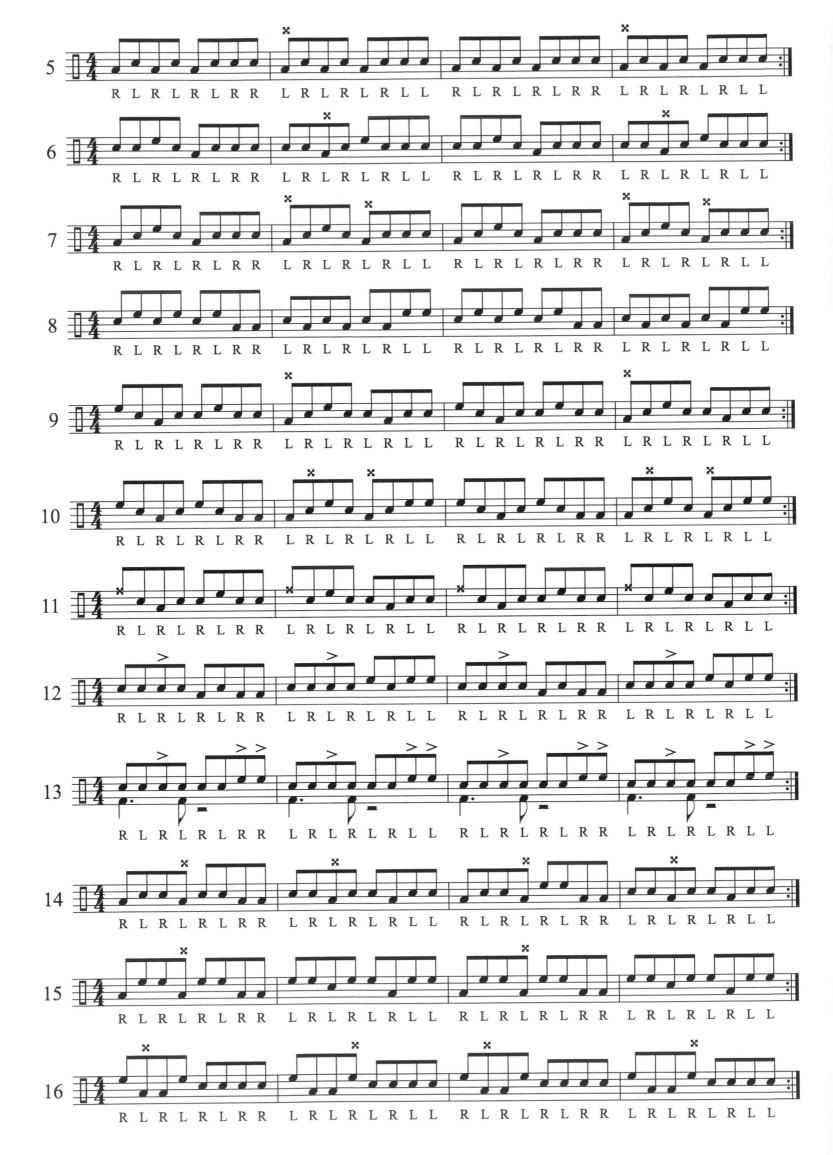

TRIPLE RATAMACUE

Each exercise is to be preceded by four measures of time.

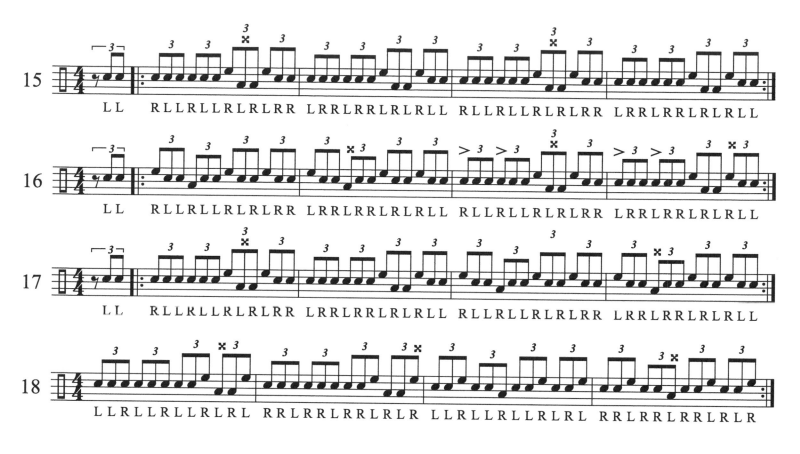

15 L L | R L L R L L R L R L R R | L R R L R R L R L R L L | R L L R L L R L R L R R | L R R L R R L R L R L L

16 L L | R L L R L L R L R L R R | L R R L R R L R L R L L | R L L R L L R L R L R R | L R R L R R L R L R L L

17 L L | R L L R L L R L R L R R | L R R L R R L R L R L L | R L L R L L R L R L R R | L R R L R R L R L R L L

18 L L R L L R L L R L R L | R R L R R L R R L R L R | L L R L L R L L R L R L | R R L R R L R R L R L R

COMBINATIONS OF VARIOUS RUDIMENTS

This section is designed to show you how to combine various rudiments. After practicing the exercises from here to the end of the book, go back to the beginning sections and make up exercises using material from different parts. In this way you will develop a vast vocabulary. Here's an example utilizing the long roll and single paradiddles.

1A R R L L R R L L | R R L L R R L L | R L R R L R L L | R L R R L R L L

1B R R L L R R L L | R R L L R R L L | R R L L R R L L R R L L | R R L L R R L L R R L L

1C R L R R L R L L | R L R R L R L L | R R L L R R L L R R L L | R R L L R R L L R R L L

1D R R L L R R L L | R R L L R R L L | R L R R L R L L R L R R | L R L L R L R R L R L L

1E R R L L R R L L | R R L L R R L L | R L R R L R L L R L R R L R | L L R L R R L R L L

These exercises use paradiddles and flam accents.

This one combines single, double, and triple paradiddles.

These exercises use single flam paradiddles and five-stroke rolls.

EIGHT-BAR PHRASE

Here's a combination of five- and seven-stroke rolls and single paradiddles.

LLRRLRRLLRLL RRLLRLLRRLLR LLRRLRRLLRLL RRLLRLLRRLLR

LRLLRLRRLLRRLR RLLRLLRRLRRLL RLRRLRLLRRLLRL LRRLRRLLRLRLL

This exercise combines seven- and nine-stroke rolls, long rolls, and single paradiddles.

RR LL RR LL R LLRRLLR RRL LRRL LRLL

RLRRLRLL RRLLRRLLRRLL RLRRLRLLRLRRLRLL RLRRLRLLRLRRLRLL

This exercise has seven-stroke rolls and single and double paradiddles.

RLRRLRLL RLRRLRLL RLRRLRLL RLRRLRLL

RLRRLRLLR L R L RRLRLRLL RLRRLRLL LLRRLL

SIXTEEN-BAR PHRASE

These short roll combinations utilize five-, seven-, and nine-stroke rolls. Accents may be played with the bass drum.

RRLLRRL RRLLR LLRRL RRLLRRL

RRLLR LLRRL RRLLRRLLR LLRRL RRLLRRLLR LLRRL

RRLLRRL RRLLRRLLR RRLLRRL RRLLR

RRLLR LLRRL RRLLR LLRRLLR RRLLRRLLRRLLRRLL

RRLLRRLLRRLLRRL RRLLRRL RRLLR LLRRL RRLL

EXERCISES ON IMPROVISING

The exercises in the rest of the book give you a chance to express your own ideas. Play the first half of the exercise as written, and then improvise for the remainder of the phrase.